The Busy Woman
Gluten-Free

By Theresa Crouse

Acknowledgements

To my dear baby sister Jennifer, who inspires me just by being the wonderful human being that she is: you make the world, and me, better. I love you.

The Busy Woman's Guide to Gluten-Free Living

Table of Contents

Contents

Preface

Hello! Thanks for buying my book! Before we get started, I want to say in advance that I'm not a doctor though I've written for them many times in the land of ghost-writing. For the last several years, I've been the starving researcher and ghostwriter behind more than 20 eBooks about various health topics.

The one opinion that all of those clients shared was the illogical insistence that each book be painfully long in order to "give readers value." Well, what if the value comes from not NEEDING to take a week to find out what you need to know? What about people who are busy? What about those of us who just want the info without the fluff so that we can learn what we need to learn and then get on with life?

That's when the idea for the "Busy Woman's Guide" series struck me. I'm going to tell you everything that you need to know, with no excess BS, in a format short enough to read though quickly. Then I'm going to give you some recipes that will (hopefully) stimulate your creativity and get your gluten-free juices flowing.

I'll even offer up some opinions on products and substitutions that I've used in order to help you find good stuff and avoid wasting time and money on garbage. That stuff's not cheap even when it does taste like crap!

I chose this topic as the first in my "Busy Woman's Guide" series because I've been diagnosed with non-celiac gluten sensitivity. Learning to live with it hasn't been an easy journey. That's why I decided to write this book - to shorten the learning curve a bit for somebody else. I hope it helps.

Chapter 1

What the Heck is Gluten, Anyway?

Before we get started, you should know what, exactly, it is that you're trying to avoid. Bear with me for a minute because this may sound a tad stuffy, but I'll be quick about it. If you're serious about going gluten-free, then this is stuff you need to know because gluten isn't just in bread.

Gluten is a composite term used to refer to the two proteins (gliadin and glutenin) found in wheat, barley, rye and triticale, a hybrid of wheat and rye. There are several different varieties of wheat including today's commercial product that's been hybridized to the point of namelessness, as well as durum, spelt, farina, kamut, khorasan, faro, and even the ancient wheat, einkorn. Sometimes the protein in corn or rice will be referred to as gluten, but it's not the same thing.

Gluten in Bread

Gluten gives bread its elasticity, helps it to rise, makes it chewy and keeps it from being crumbly. The more gluten there is in the dough (or the more refined it is), the chewier it will be - think bagels and pizza dough. Typically, bread doughs are higher in gluten while pastry doughs are lower; thus the lighter, more delicate texture of pastries.

There are many ways that bakers manipulate gluten content to alter textures but that's beyond the scope of our conversation, since we're going to be avoiding gluten altogether. The important thing to know is that traditional commercial breads and pastries contain some amount of gluten, so avoid them like the plague.

Don't worry too much though: I'm going to give you some work-arounds so that baked goods can remain a delicious part of life if you want them to be. Personally, I've enjoyed the butt shrinkage that has accompanied giving them up (nearly) altogether, but that's up to you!

Gluten in Food

Most restaurant sauces, dips and gravies and even nacho cheese contain flour as the thickener because it's cheap, convenient, and easy to use. It also keeps well so it just makes sense for cooks to use it. That's bad for us, though, because it means that all of those products are off-limits to us.

This list often includes tortilla chips so be careful ordering nachos or dips with chips because you'll quite likely double-dose yourself between the flour in the dip or cheese and the flour in the chips. Be careful when eating out because the tiniest bit of flour may be enough to make you miserable, and you'll spend the day sick and wondering what happened.

Extracted Gluten

Just like whey or soy proteins, gluten can be extracted from wheat, dried and milled so that it can be used in a basically pure form for other purposes. For instance, bakers add extra gluten to flour to get chewier products with a more stable structure, or to make it rise more. Extracted gluten also thickens sauces and adds protein and flavor to products such as processed foods and artificial meats that are favorites of many vegetarians.

Cooks also dust extracted gluten onto meats or other foods that are difficult to bread. If the breading won't stick, dusting it in gluten first will help. Of course, if the product is breaded with wheat flour, there's gluten in that too.

Finally, flour and gluten are commonly used as thickening agents and to keep products such as spice mixes from caking. We'll touch on this more in Chapter 4. If you're like I was, you're going to be surprised by some of the places that wheat and gluten are hiding.

Chapter 2

The Rise in Gluten Intolerance

For the last several decades, there has been a substantial increase in cases of wheat-related conditions. This increase is too great to be attributed to better reporting and diagnostic methods, so scientists are trying to nail down the cause. The findings so far have often been less than conclusive and the more that is discovered, the more questions arise.

Why Are So Many People Suddenly Becoming Sensitive to Gluten?

The funny thing about the sudden rise in gluten intolerance is that for centuries, we've eaten grains with relatively few problems. Why is it starting to bother so many people now? Two reasons are being targeted: genetic modification and milling methods.

Scientists have been messing with our food in the name of efficiency and profit, and food manufacturers have gotten away from using freshly milled wheat in favor of heavily processing it in order to get the most bang for their buck.

Not that it's any big surprise, but in an effort to create a bigger crop in a smaller space or to get that light, fluffy bread texture that's so popular, scientists and farmers have been messing around with wheat

DNA (and most other big-money crops) for about the last 60 years or so.

During the Green Revolution that occurred post-WWII, scientists started fiddling with hybridizing different types of wheat in order to increase yield and disease resistance. The movement was led by a guy named Norman Borlaug, who actually won the Nobel Peace Prize for "saving 1 billion lives."

One of the initiatives that he led developed a new, high-yielding species of a semi-dwarf wheat that, when grown with certain pesticides and fertilizers, increased wheat yield exponentially. The goal of solving world hunger was met but many believe that it was at the cost of the nutritional value of wheat.

With the invention of the steel roller mill in the 1870's, white flour because easy and cheap to produce. It was so popular that within a decade, all stone mills in the western world were gone.

Steel roller milling removes the bran, germ, and other parts of the kernel that contain the most vitamins, lipids, minerals, and proteins. All it leaves behind is the white powdery part that is nearly devoid of nutrition but packed full of gluten and empty carbohydrates. It sure does taste good, though.

As a result of hybridization and steel roller milling, the flour of today is drastically different than the flour of the early 1900's, both in the way that the wheat is grown and in the way that it's prepared.

There appears to be a debate about an actual increase in gluten content in this new wheat, but the practice of adding more gluten to flour and to foods at various stages of preparation can't be denied.

Scientists speculate that it's this combination of excess gluten use, steel roller milling, and genetic modification that is causing so many more cases of celiac disease, wheat allergy, and gluten sensitivity. I t's not particularly surprising that this new product doesn't agree with many of us; we've taken a nutritious, wholesome product and mutated it, soaked it in poison, grown it in chemicals, and milled all of the nutrition out of it. Yum.

But Still, Why Wheat?

The bottom line is that sensitivities and allergies related to wheat aren't well-understood yet. For the 1% of the population that suffers from celiac disease, it's cut and dried: gluten is the root of all evil. For others of us, though, it's not so cut and dried. Is it gluten? Is it something else in the wheat?

Whatever it is, going gluten-free provides relief of symptoms, so that's what we do. It's one of those cases where the more we learn, the more we realize that we don't know. Progress thus far has been slow and painful, but it IS being made.

Chapter 3

What's the Difference Between Celiac Disease, Wheat Allergy, and Non-Celiac Gluten Sensitivity?

These terms are often tossed about almost interchangeably but there are significant differences both in symptoms and in function. They are as different from each other as a cold and an ingrown toenail, except for they share similar symptoms and a common factor, at least in part. "Gluten intolerance" is typically used as an umbrella term to describe all three ailments.

Celiac Disease

Celiac disease is an autoimmune disease (more correctly, it's a T-cell-mediated immune reaction with an auto-immune component, but who's getting that scientific?) that affects the digestive process in the small intestine. It's often inherited and damages the lining of the intestine, disrupting nutrient absorption and causing severe digestive upset including cramps, bloating and diarrhea.

Celiac disease can be medically diagnosed using an intestinal biopsy and blood screening. There are currently several medicines in the research stage that may prove useful in treating it. For now, absolute avoidance of gluten is the only effective way to remain healthy.

Because gluten actually damages the lining of the intestine, people with celiac disease may need to supplement with vitamins even after going gluten-free in order to make up for the nutrients that can't be absorbed by the small intestine.

Reactions to gluten (specifically glutenins and gliadin) is slow and may take anywhere from 30 minutes to 24 hours to appear because food must reach the small intestine in order to stimulate a reaction.

Eating gluten causes damage to the intestine each time that it's ingested. This happens because the immune system incorrectly identifies gluten proteins as foreign invaders and mounts a response. Unfortunately, it doesn't just attack the proteins; it also attacks the lining of your gut. Over time, this causes leaky gut, tremendous inflammation, and has even been linked to cancer.

Reactions to gluten vary in intensity from person to person, or depending upon how much gluten was consumed and may include:

- Heartburn
- IBS
- Stomach cramps
- Bloating
- Vomiting
- Diarrhea
- Nausea
- Fever
- Fatigue
- Sweating
- Cold chills
- Respiratory issues
- Sneezing
- Itching
- Rashes, red skin, or hives
- Eczema or psoriasis
- Brain fog
- Headaches
- Joint Pain and arthritis

Wheat Allergy/Gluten Allergy

An allergic reaction to wheat is also an autoimmune response, but it's not a disease. There is no long-term damage and reactions can be completely avoided by avoiding wheat. Essentially, if you're allergic to wheat, your body incorrectly recognizes it as a pathogen and initiates an immune response to get rid of it.

Just a note: according to most credible sources, there is no recognized allergy to gluten. There's "non-celiac gluten sensitivity" and then there's wheat allergy. Of course, there's the other side of the battle that claims that a reaction to wheat is actually a reaction to the gluten.

Again, there are still so many unknown factors that a solid answer has yet to be found.

Wheat allergies can be diagnosed with an allergy test called a RAST or with skin- prick testing. Double-blind placebo testing can also be used for diagnosis as long as you're not one of those people who experience severe anaphylactic symptoms such as respiratory problems or swelling of the throat.

Allergic reactions to wheat occur quickly, within minutes to a few hours, and vary in intensity. For some, the reaction may be deadly, but for others may include only minor irritation. Symptoms are the same as those for any food allergy and include:

- IBS
- Fever
- Sweating
- Chills
- Fatigue
- Sneezing
- Runny nose

- Respiratory difficulties such as asthma, swelling of the throat, or difficulty breathing/talking
- Muscle stiffness or swelling
- Joint pain or swelling
- Rashes, hives, or redness
- Eczema or psoriasis (this is more chronic)
- Headaches
- Brain fog or confusion
- Low blood pressure
- Nausea
- Vomiting
- Diarrhea
- Unconsciousness
- Death
- Anaphylaxis – a combination of two or more of these symptoms at once, with rapid onset.

Though these symptoms may appear to be similar to those of celiac disease, remember that the onset is rapid and that they can go from bad to worse quickly depending upon your immune response. If you start to experience any sort of difficulty breathing, you should get to a hospital. Carrying an Epi-Pen isn't a bad idea, either.

Non-Celiac Gluten Sensitivity or Intolerance (NCGS)

This condition is hotly contested in the medical world; some say it exists while others say that it's a form of wheat allergy or even a psychological response. Rest assured though, coming from somebody who's living it: it's a real condition.

Diagnostic testing for it is differential, which just means that after you test negative for celiac disease and wheat allergy, they put you on a gluten-free diet. If your symptoms disappear, then you're officially diagnosed.

Not really scientific, but since the mechanics of the condition are still a mystery, it's the best that they have right now. Research estimates that 18 million Americans suffer from NCGS, about eight times the number of people with celiac disease.

I have this, and it's frustrating because sometimes I can eat a small amount of gluten without becoming symptomatic, but at other times, even trace amounts make me miserable. Since they don't know what the exact culprit is, I just have to stay away from it altogether if I don't want my stomach sounding (and feeling) like it's experiencing a cat-5 earthquake.

I'm eagerly awaiting new findings but until they get a better handle on the entire gluten/wheat issue, I'll go without, thanks very much. Another interesting point that I've discovered is that, the longer I'm gluten-free, the sicker I get if I cheat. Something to ponder, I guess.

Just as with a wheat allergy, NCGS doesn't cause permanent damage to your intestines. Instead, you suffer from the symptoms for up to a couple of days, and then you feel better again. Unlike an allergy, it isn't fatal. You may WISH for death while you're sick, but trust me, it won't actually kill you.

Symptom onset is slow and, like allergies or celiac disease, will vary from person to person or incident to incident. Here are the symptoms for NCGS:

- IBS
- Heart burn
- Stomach cramps
- Nausea
- Vomiting
- Diarrhea
- Bloating
- Fever

- Fatigue
- Chills
- Respiratory issues
- Runny nose
- Arthritis (chronic)
- Itching, hives, redness or swelling of your skin
- Eczema or psoriasis (chronic)
- Brain fog
- Headaches/migraines (chronic)

You've probably noticed that the symptoms to all 3 conditions are similar. Onset times vary, but all basically mess up your digestive system as expected. What's not entirely expected are the other problems such as joint pain and brain fog, but those were actually the two symptoms that sent me to the doctor. Now that I've been studying the condition ad nauseam, that's a pretty common situation.

Just a note: If you're planning to be tested for celiac disease, do not stop eating gluten before the test because it can (and most probably will) lead to a false negative. You have to have gluten in your system for the test to be accurate.

Other Illnesses and Conditions Related to Gluten

The gluten-free market is exploding, and it isn't just because of us folks with some form of gluten intolerance. As research advances and more studies are done upon various major illnesses, gluten is being considered as a factor.

In several situations, gluten antibodies were found in a significant portion of people suffering from these conditions. When a gluten-free diet was prescribed, many people began to see a lessening of symptoms.

Here are a few examples of diseases or complications that have been linked, at least tentatively, to gluten:

- **Arthritis**
- **Rheumatoid arthritis** – there are actually some exciting studies going on here!
- **Cerebellar ataxia** – a neurological disorder believed to be at least partially caused by gluten
- **Certain subsets of schizophrenia**
- **Autism** – study here is still new but suggests that GF diets may help in certain situations.
- **Epilepsy** – some patients report significant improvement after going GF.
- **Psoriasis**
- **Eczema**
- **Unexplained migraines**
- **Low blood pressure**
- **Brain fog**
- **Unexplained allergy symptoms** such as rash or hives, runny nose, and breathing problems.

The bottom line is that, since it's known that gluten causes a rise in disease-causing inflammation at least in people who are sensitive to it, people are avoiding it like the plague in the name of health.

Though some doctors say that wheat is a vital part of the human diet, it really isn't. You can get all of the vitamins, minerals and nutrients that are in grain (and there aren't that many nowadays) in other, less questionable, healthier food.

I'm not telling you that wheat is horrible if you aren't sensitive to it. I'm just pointing out that many people have made the decision to forego gluten for reasons other than intolerance.

Now that you know the basics about gluten and the different types of gluten intolerances, let's move on and talk about foods and products that contain gluten.

Chapter 4

Gluten Sources - You're Going to be Surprised!

Standard breads, crackers and pastas contain gluten, so if you just skip those or buy gluten-free versions, you'll be fine, right? Wrong! Remember how we talked about the different ways that gluten is used? It's in so many products that the only way to really be sure that you're not inadvertently eating it is to read the labels.

Eating out can be a challenge in the beginning but most restaurants offer gluten-free menus. However, some of them are really skimpy, so once you get a feel for what you can eat and what you can't, you can start manipulating the menu to meet your needs. For example, you can always change out sides, dressings or gravies. It's just a matter of getting the hang of it.

I included a brief guide to eating out at the end of this book to help you get started.

The No-No List

These are foods that you need to avoid unless they're labeled gluten-free or you check the label:

Beer – yup. Sorry. Unless it's labeled GF, beer contains gluten.
Bread
Breaded foods
Crackers
Frozen processed meats and meat products

Frozen veggies with sauce mixes – gluten or flour is often the thickener.

Gravy – it's thickened with flour.

Imitation crab meat – uses flour as a binding agent.

Malt vinegar – most malt vinegars contain wheat.

Many cold cereals

Miso – often made with barley.

Nacho Cheese (yup, sorry. It's usually thickened with flour.)

Pancakes, waffles

Pasta

Pastries

Pizza

Restaurant French fries – they're probably fried in the same oil as breaded products, so cross-contamination is a concern.

Seasoned or battered French fries – often the seasoning has flour or gluten.

Soy sauce

Teriyaki sauce

Veggie burgers - often contain wheat as a binding agent.

There are many foods that SOMETIMES contain gluten or wheat depending upon the brand that you buy. Here are a few products that you need to be aware of. Check the labels.

Foods on the Mighty "Maybe" List

Foods that ALWAYS have gluten and foods that are always gluten-free are generally easy to identify, but foods on the "maybe" list are quite a bit tougher. In addition to being the protein that gives bread its elasticity, gluten also used in many different products as a thickening agent, a flavor booster, a stabilizer, or a protein enhancer. This is why you need to read labels – just a few of the foods that you need to watch for this in include:

Meats

Bratwurst
Hot Dogs
Imitation Meats (i.e. imitation crab meat contains gluten)
Sausage
Vegetarian Meats

Condiments

Ketchup
Marinades
Salad Dressings
Sauces
Seasonings
Soy Sauce
Teriyaki Sauce

Snacks

Cheese Dips and other Creamy Dips
Corn Chips
French Fries
Ice Cream
Mixers, including Margarita Mix and Bloody Mary Mix
Pudding
Seasoned Chips

Cheeses

Some Cheese Spreads – just check the label
Some Cottage Cheese – Daisy and Friendship are both GF

Some Cream Cheese spreads. Plain is GF but the flavored ones may have some

Miscellaneous

Barbeque sauce – some, not all.
Candy – some (Twizzlers for example) contain gluten or wheat.
Canned or Frozen Fruits – some contain thickener
Canned or Frozen Vegetables – some contain thickeners
Canned soups – may use wheat-based thickeners.
Chewing gum – some brands use flour to keep them from sticking to the paper.
Chocolate – don't freak out. Only some of them contain gluten or flour as a binder or thickener.
Commercial Soups – read your labels.
Deli meats – depends on the brand but many use it as a filler or flavoring.
Drink mixers – particularly bloody Mary mixes and margarita mixes often have gluten.
Flavored potato chips – gluten or flour is often used in the seasoning.
Hot dogs – some do, some don't.
Ice cream – some use flour in the recipe.
Instant coffee and tea – gluten is sometimes used as a bulking agent, especially in flavored ones.
Ketchup – some use gluten or flour as a thickener. Heinz is GF.
Nacho cheese – this one broke my heart. Flour is often used as a thickener.
Pickles – some are cured in malt vinegar, which may contain gluten.
Pringles chips (Lays Stax are GF!)

Pudding – flour is often used as a thickener.

Salad dressings – gluten or flour may be used as a stabilizing agent or thickener.

Sausage and store-bought meatballs – often contain wheat as a binder.

Spices and spice blends – gluten is frequently used as an anti-caking agent. Curry powder is a good example.

Store-bought or restaurant sauces – again, thickener.

Tortilla chips – chips used to make nachos or chips and salsa in restaurants are often flour tortilla chips, not corn chips.

Vitamins and medications – gluten is often used as a binding agent.

Worcestershire sauce – sometimes contains barley malt vinegar. Heinz is GF.

You don't have to avoid these foods altogether because there are many that are perfectly gluten-free. Just read your labels and pay attention. Just a heads up: blue cheese has long been considered a gluten-containing food because of the way that it's made but recent testing has shown that the finished product meets the guidelines for gluten-free labeling.

Many companies voluntarily include a statement at the end of the ingredients list that includes allergens, but this isn't mandatory. The best way to ensure that your food is gluten-free is to read your labels.

You have to be especially careful because just because wheat isn't listed as an ingredient, there are many other ingredients that contain gluten. If you see any of these ingredients listed on a product, assume there's gluten in it unless it's specifically labeled as gluten-free.

Artificial flavorings – gluten is sometimes used to enhance flavor.

Atta flour

Barley
Bleached Flour
Bread flour
Bulgar
Couscous
Dextrin
Farina
Hordeum vulgare (barley)
Hydrolyzed Vegetable Protein (HVP)
Malt
Modified Food Starch
Natural Flavors
Rye
Seasoning
Secale cereal (rye)
Seitan (commonly used in vegetarian meals)
Spelt
Triticale
Triticum spelta (spelt)
Triticum vulgare (wheat)
Unbleached flour
Vegetable Gum
Vegetable Protein
Vegetable Starch
Vegetable starch – sometimes made from wheat
Wheat
Wheat flour
Wheat germ oil (cross-contamination issues)
Wheat protein (hydrolyzed, too)
Wheat starch (hydrolyzed, too)

Even if a product doesn't have wheat listed in the allergens list, it never hurts to take a glance through the ingredients list for yourself just to be sure. After all, the president of the potato chip company isn't going to be sick in a few hours after eating his product so it's not quite as important to him as it is to you.

There are a ton of rumors flying around the web regarding gluten-containing ingredients, so I wanted to clear the good name of a few products, as well as expand your "can-have" list. Here are some foods that are OK regardless of rumors:

Maltodextrin – the protein is removed during processing so even if it contains wheat, it's still gluten-free. Of course, if you're allergic to wheat, you still can't have it!

Distilled alcohols – the gluten is typically removed from the alcohol during the distillation process so distilled alcohols, even those made from wheat, should be fine. Check your favorite though, just to be sure.

Caramel coloring – regardless of the hoopla, it's made from corn and is GF in the US and many other places. If you're traveling abroad, you may want to avoid it just in case.

All Boar's Head deli meats are GF.

Wheat grass and barley grass – the gluten is in the seeds, not the grass. There may be a fear of cross-contamination, though.

Many cold cereals, including Chex (except Wheat Chex).

Sourdough bread is currently being researched as safe for the gluten-sensitive and even for celiacs because the long fermentation process breaks down the gluten in the flour. It's not conclusive yet but it sure is looking promising for us!

If you're like me and don't have time to spend hours in the kitchen baking on a regular basis, relax. Because GF eating has become so popular, new products are popping up every day. It kills me that they cost so much, but welcome to the world of capitalism. Ingredients are expensive and there isn't much competition so they can basically charge what they want to. Still, it's nice to have some GF ready-made products on hand. Here are a few of my favorites:

Udi's French Baguettes and French Dinner Rolls – these are my go-to breads for just about everything. They taste good and toast well. The only real give-away that they're GF is that they're not quite as absorbent as wheat bread. If you're craving garlic bread, cinnamon toast bites or a sub, these are so good that they entire family will love them.

Udi's Bagels – Found in the GF frozen section. These are good if you like whole-grain products with seeds, etc. The only complaint that I have with the taste is that they're not salty enough for me. Besides that, they fit the bill when I want a bagel.

Udi's everything else – Found in the GF frozen section. They also offer hamburger and hotdog buns, sandwich bread, frozen dinners, muffins, cookies, pizza crusts, tortillas and granola bars, just to name a few. I haven't tried everything on the list yet but what I have tried, I've liked, and I'm picky. I particularly like the tortillas because I really hate the "off the shelf" alternative, corn tortillas.

Rudi's cinnamon raisin bread – home run. Keep it in the freezer and just thaw out what you need though.

Rudi's products – they have sandwich bread, hamburger buns, tortillas, ciabatta rolls, stuffing and pizza crusts. They're all OK but again aren't as absorbent as wheat breads and the texture is a bit off, too. The sandwich bread is OK but just isn't as moist as wheat bread and breaks easily. I like it best for toast.

Hint: When you buy frozen breads of any sort, leave them in the freezer until you're ready to use them or they'll get a weird taste and texture. I leave the sandwich bread and buns in the freezer and pull them out a few slices at a time, then just defrost in the microwave or toaster.

Thai Kitchen Instant Rice Noodle Soup – I confess: I'm a ramen noodle fan. These are a great substitution and come in three different flavors: Bangkok Curry, Garlic and Vegetable and Spring Onion. They're good but be careful not to overcook them. With rice noodles there's a fine line between ready-to-eat and glue.

LivingGFree – I've tried their crackers, pizza dough, brownie mix, pre-made snickerdoodles, granola, frozen pizza and chicken nuggets. The crackers, dough, cookies, granola and brownie mix are fabulous! The frozen pizza and chicken nuggets were good, but not as good as the first three. However, I'm a repeat buyer, and your kids seriously won't know the difference with the nuggets.

Glutino GF Chocolate Vanilla Cream Cookies – Oreo cookie lovers take note. These will cure your cookie craving in a hurry. They're even delightfully dunkable. As a matter of fact, most of Glutino's sweets are decent.

Van's GF Waffles – even the college kids in my house like these. So much so that I shove them to the back of the freezer so that I may actually stand a chance of getting one. They have regular and blueberry; both are great.

Sam Mills Pasta D'Oro – corn pasta that comes in a variety of shapes. It tastes good and takes sauces well. Rinse it as soon as it's done cooking or else you'll get starchy goop.

Betty Crocker GF cake and brownie mixes – For the most part, all of these are delicious. The early attempts weren't so great but they've finally gotten the hang of it.

The "Not Quite There Yet" List

There are also a few items that have made my "eww list" that I'd like to share.

Schar GF shortbread cookies – dry and have a gritty texture. They taste sort of like the box after you drop it in sand.

Glutino parmesan and garlic bagel chips – the flavoring, which is extremely garlicy, is only on the outside so the actual chip is bland. They're also really hard. The do make decent croutons though.

Udi's cinnamon rolls – super hard and tasted stale right out of the box.

Kinnikininnick vanilla glazed donuts – I wasn't sure if I was eating the donut or the box.

Rice bread – weird texture, weirder taste. I've never tasted a rice bread that I found even remotely palatable.

I'm just offering my opinion here; it could be that you'll love what I hate so if you want to try it for yourself, go for it. Also, companies change recipes so hopefully those on the eww list will get it right eventually.

None of these lists are exhaustive but at least it's a start. Just read your labels until you get the hang of it and get to know the ingredients in your favorite products. If you're eating out, don't be afraid to ask your server to check the ingredients for you. They're usually good about it.

It won't take long before you're a pro and picking out gluten-containing foods will become second nature.

Chapter 5

Cooking Without Gluten: Handy Tricks and Tips

Cooking without gluten takes some getting used to but it's not as big a transition as you may think. Unless you're a huge baker, you'll only need to make some (mostly) minor tweaks to the way that you do things.

Fortunately, there are some really great GF products out there that are so good that you won't really miss out on much once you learn how to use them. Here are a few tips:

- Sift or stir your dry ingredients together really well to avoid pockets of one type of flour.
- Use eggs. They add moisture, act as a leavener and help hold the product together. Try replacing 1/2 cup of the water or other liquid with 1/2 cup of eggs or egg whites.
- Mix all ingredients together in one bowl and whip plenty of air into it. This will help activate your leaveners and add lightness to your product.
- Use all ingredients at room temperature unless expressly directed otherwise. This actually applies to regular baking as well as GF baking. Egg whites whip better and butter combines more evenly.
- Consider using soda water instead of regular water to give your product a bit more lightness and volume.

- Toss a teaspoon of fruit pectin into your dough to keep the final product moist. Using applesauce in place of some of the oil in cookies or muffins helps with this too.
- Be sure to clean all of your equipment and your workspace well in order to prevent cross-contamination of gluten. If possible, have tools and a workspace dedicated to GF cooking only.
- Use a combination of starches, medium flours and heavy flours to get the most lift, texture and structure in your baked goods. They all have specific properties that complement each other and work best in tandem.

Be creative! Just like with regular baking, don't be afraid to try new things. In the beginning, don't change more than one ingredient or technique at once so that you know what caused the change but once you get the basics, don't be afraid to get a little freaky!

Thickeners

If you like to make such things as mashed potatoes and gravy, Salisbury steak or roux-based sauces, you have several options that replace white flour as the thickener so well that you won't even miss it.

Cornstarch – Thecolor of your sauce will be a bit different – it'll be clearer and glossier – but the taste will be pretty much spot-on. Make a slurry by adding 1 tablespoon of milk or water to 1 tablespoon of cornstarch, then add it to your liquid.

One tablespoon of cornstarch thickens 1 cup of liquid. If you're using a recipe, replace the flour with half the amount of cornstarch. 1 tablespoon of cornstarch = 2 tablespoons of flour.

Cornstarch is great to use if you're going to be eating the sauce or gravy immediately but it gets gelatinous after it sits for a bit. In my opinion, it's the best thickener for dairy-based sauces but it doesn't work quite so well in acidic recipes. It warms up OK from the fridge (though a bit gelatinous) but it doesn't freeze well. Also, be sure not to overcook it or else it will get a little pasty in texture.

Arrowroot Starch – I actually prefer this to wheat flour in acidic recipes such as stews. It's made from tubers from the West Indies. Just make a slurry with equal parts water and arrowroot, then add it to your liquid. Stir over medium heat until it's thick.

Use about 1 tablespoon of arrowroot per 1 cup of liquid when figuring how much you'll need to make your sauce. If you're following a recipe, replace the flour with half the amount of arrowroot. 2 tablespoons of flour = 1 tablespoon of arrowroot.

Arrowroot stands up well to reheating and freezing but be careful using it in dairy-based sauces because it may get a bit slimy. It's great in dessert sauces such as cherry pies.

Tapioca Starch – First, let's define the difference between tapioca starch and tapioca flour. Often, there is no difference because some manufacturers lump both products under the same name but sometimes flour is ground more coarsely than starch. If not, then they are essentially the same thing and may be substituted for one another.

To tell the difference, just look at it. If it looks like a fine powder, then you have tapioca starch, regardless of what it's labeled.

There's also instant tapioca and tapioca pearls that can be used. Personally, I don't like the pearls unless I'm making tapioca pudding because they often don't dissolve completely. That's how tapioca pudding should be, but I prefer my pie filling free of blobby chunks, thanks.

Tapioca starch is great when you want to thicken something at the last minute. It thickens quickly and at a relatively low temperature. Goods thickened with tapioca also freeze well so feel free to make an extra pie or five for later while you're baking!

Potato Starch – If you're a lover of thick, creamy soups like chowders, you'll probably love potato starch. It's my go-to thickener for those types of recipes because it's not gritty, it doesn't alter the flavor and you can add it at the end by simply making a slurry and adding it to the pot.

Use 1 tablespoon of potato starch for each cup of liquid. A word of warning: don't ever boil your liquid after you add potato starch to it because it won't thicken properly.

Potato starch is exactly what the name implies: an extremely fine powder made from the starchy part of potatoes. You can use even if you're allergic to corn or are on a grain-free diet and it's Passover-friendly.

DO NOT mistake potato FLOUR for potato starch because they are two vastly different animals. We'll talk about potato flour in the baking section.

Buying tip: If you have an Asian market nearby, you can find potato starch for a buck or so for a small bag. Your regular grocery store will probably charge more.

Kudzu Powder – Made from a vine native to Japan, Kudzu is now growing out of control all over the South. It comes in chunks that you have to grind yourself and acts in the same way that cornstarch does. It has several reputed health benefits but is usually wicked expensive. I don't use it myself but it's an option.

Use 1 1/2 tablespoons of powder for each cup of liquid. Make a slurry of equal parts kudzu powder and cold water then simmer for a few minutes to allow it to thicken.

Sweet Rice Flour – This is made from short-grain rice, which is the kind that you use to make sticky rice. It has a high starch content which is what make it work as a thickener. Despite the name, it's not sweet; it's actually kind of milky flavored.

You can use this to make a roux just like you would use regular flour. I don't like to use it (or regular rice flour for that matter) because it leaves a gritty feeling in my mouth no matter how finely it's ground.

Guar Gum – Many people use guar gum as a thickener for gravies and sauces but I'm not a fan. It has a propensity to get slimy, which is gross.

A Few Final Words about Thickeners

This is an area where it's all about personal preference. Personally, I prefer corn starch, arrowroot or tapioca starch for my sauces. You can also buy several different really good types of GF flour from most any major retailer.

I've been a fan of thickening with corn starch, and more recently tapioca starch and arrowroot, for too long to be in any hurry to try different GF flours for thickening. It's up to you though. You may as well give them all a chance if for no other reason than process of elimination. Find out what you like and go with it.

Gluten-Free Baking Flours

This one's a bit tricky because what kind of flour you use, and what you add to it, is dependent upon the flavor and texture that you're shooting for. I'm going to tell you about the most popular flours and commercial mixes and what they're best used for. Then you can feel free to experiment for yourself because there really is no substitute for experience.

Just a note: GF flours are completely different than wheat flours. Your pancake, waffle and muffin mixes are often going to be thicker than their wheat-laden counterparts because many GF flours are much more absorbent than wheat flour is. On the other hand, your bread dough may resemble pancake batter. It's OK. It may not look right but before you go adding more liquid or flour, cook it or bake it as-is the first time.

You may want to use GF recipes written specifically for the type of flour that you're using instead of trying to modify standard recipes until you get a good feel for the properties of your ingredients.

Commercial Baking Mixes

Sometimes it's nice to just reach into the cabinet and grab a bag of flour. If you're not a big baker, then this may be the best option for you. I do like to bake but sometimes I just don't feel like mixing my own. That's why I keep some commercial mixes on hand. For the most part, though, I prefer to use my own mixes because I can adapt them to suit the recipe.

Allergen Warning: Commercial baking mixes often contain nut or bean flours so if you have an allergy to either, beware.

Bisquick Gluten-Free Pancake and Baking Mix – This is my latest new toy for when I'm in a hurry. As a southern girl, pancakes and biscuits have always been on my list of favorite treats and this mix is really good, especially considering that it's made with rice flour.

It's not grainy and side-by-side, the pancakes are just as good as those made with wheat flour. You can use it for breading, cakes and gravy, too. Betty Crocker has a ton of great recipes on their site for it. The downside is that it's a bit pricey. You can always make the mix yourself from scratch if you have the time.

Some tips: Beware that there's no oil or shortening in it. I messed up the first time that I made biscuits because I didn't read the directions. I just added water to it like I always did with regular Bisquick and the results were terrible. Also, if you let it sit for a few minutes after it's mixed, you'll get a lighter, fluffier product.

Pamela's Ultimate Baking and Pancake Mix is excellent, too. There are only two reasons that I rank it second instead of first: it's sometimes tough to find where I'm at and it's pricey.

Bob's Red Mill Baking Flours – I really like Bob's Red Mill all-purpose flour for waffles, breading and baking. The all-purpose and baking flours are fairly affordable, especially when you compare them to nut flours and they're not grainy.

Many recipes actually call for these flours because they're the go-to products for people who don't want to mix their own. There are a couple of different bean flours in it though so if you can't do beans, then this isn't the mix for you.

Bob's Red Mill Cornbread Mix – I love this mix. It tastes just like regular cornbread, though I do prefer to add a bit more salt and sugar to it. Nobody that tastes this ever knows that it's GF. It's a bit thicker than my old favorite Jiffy cornbread mix but other than that, you won't notice much of a difference. **Hodgson Mill** and **Stonewall Kitchens** has a good cornbread mix, too.

Tip: Let it stand for a few minutes after you mix it before you add it to your pan or to your muffin tin for a lighter cornbread.

Other Good GF Brands – There are several reliably good GF brands out there besides Bob's Red Mill or **Hodgson Mill**.

Pamela's, Glutinoand even some of the big name cake mix companies are offering good products. Because there are so many regional products, it's tough to name them all, or even all the good ones.

Mixing Your Own Flours

Mixing your own flours is a bit of an art form. In other words, you're going to have to play with the different types of flours to figure out what combination best meets your needs. GF flours come in 3 weights: Light/starchy, all-purpose medium and heavy (which roughly equates to whole-grain flour in texture). The key is to blend them in a manner that gives you the texture and rise that you're looking for.

Tip: Densities of non-wheat flours differ from standard all-purpose flour so it's usually best to weigh it instead of measure it when you're making substitutions.

Note: There's a huge difference between flour and meal when it comes to baking, but it's a simple difference. Flours are ground finely whereas meals are courser and may still have chunks of the nut or seed.

Sometimes this difference is negligible but sometimes, as when baking breads or cakes, it's significant. Don't mix them up if a recipe calls for one or the other specifically.

Light and starchy flours, such as sweet rice flour, potato flour and many of the starches that we discussed above add lightness and tenderness to your baked goods. They also serve as binding agents to prevent crumbling. You won't use but a small amount of light and starchy flours or else you'll have a gummy, gloppy mess that won't cook through. Think of them as additives rather than primary ingredients.

Sweet rice flour is good to use to add moisture and density to your recipes. You can't use it alone though or else you'll get a gloppy sludge.

Potato flour is made from whole potatoes that have been dried and ground into flour. It's extremely absorbent and will suck the moisture right up in your recipes. It's good to use in small quantities when you want to add some lightness to your recipes but use it sparingly. You can use it in place of xanthan gum in your recipes.

Adding a bit of **potato starch** to your breads will give them a light, soft, tender texture but it won't brown well. Unlike potato bread, it ADDS moisture to your recipe. **Tapioca starch**, on the other hand, is heavier and tougher but lends a beautiful brown crust. I like to use a bit of each to get the best of both worlds.

All-purpose medium weight flours such as oat flour, brown rice flour and sorghum flour are good to use as the base, primary flour for baked goods. They share physical similarities to all-purpose wheat flour and are pretty easy to work with.

Remember though that there's no gluten in them so you'll need to add something (or a few somethings) to it give your baked goods rise and texture.

I tend to stay away from **brown rice flour** for two reasons: first, it has fairly high levels of arsenic and I try to avoid that in my diet when possible (duh). Also, since it's made with the hull of the rice kernel, it has a ricey flavor and a texture similar to whole grain flour. Since I make mostly desserts, that's not a quality that I find favorable.

Sorghum Flour, aka milo or jowar flour, is full-flavored and perhaps the closest to tasting like wheat. You can buy red or white sorghum. Both are high in protein so they lend elasticity to your doughs.

Sorghum flour is a good all-purpose flour for just about anything that you're baking or cooking including pancakes, breads, cakes, muffins or tough cookies like gingerbread or brown sugar cookies. A bonus is that it's nutritious, too.

Use it to replace up to 25-30% of your flour blend.

Tip: It bakes dark and has a rich, wheaty flavor so if your end goal is a light-colored, gently flavored product, this isn't the flour that you want to use.

Teff flour is milled from a small seed that is used as a primary source of nutrition for Ethiopians. It has a high level of protein and calcium. Teff has a mildly nutty flavor and gives a nice elasticity and structure to your baked goods.

Use it for up to 25% of your flour blend to make delicious pancakes, waffles, cakes, cookies, breads and muffins. The nutty flavor really shines through so if that's not the flavor profile that you're going for, you may want to use something else.

White rice flour is a medium-weight flour. It has a gummier texture and is sometimes grainy, at least to me. Though it's the primary ingredient in GF Bisquick, I haven't had as much luck cooking with white rice flour on my own. The one exception here is pie crusts. It makes a KILLER pie crust that will rival Great Aunt Nellie's.

Finely ground white rice flour is good for cookies or other fragile baked goods. Medium grind is what's most readily available and is usually acceptable for other kinds of baking but it may add a gritty texture. It's easy enough to grind it finer if you have a grinder or food processor.

Rice flour is pretty dense. Mix it with other flours to avoid heavy, gritty baked goods and stick with the finer grind if you can get it or make it.

Tapioca flour makes a decent hot roll and can be subbed into other recipes that call for AP flour. Use up to 50% tapioca flour in your bread recipes with the remainder being a heavier flour. It mixes well with nut flours. Some recipes use tapioca flour only. Just play with it.

Heavy flours add protein and texture to your bread. Since they tend to be higher in protein, they also help lend a bit of elasticity. This doesn't equate to rise, though. When making baked goods that you want to be light and somewhat crumbly, you need to add lighter flours and starches to counteract the density of heavier flours. Here are the most popular heavy flours available:

Nut flours and **nut meals** are made by blanching and drying nuts, then grinding them. Meals are courser and flours are ground finer. They're packed with protein and add moisture but are extremely dense. They make great pie crusts. Many recipes call for almond, hazelnut, pistachio or macadamia flours. In addition to making flavorful cakes and crusts, they're good to dredge meats in, too.

I love cooking with nut flours because they're healthy and lend a delicious nuttiness to muffins and cakes but the price can be prohibitive. I use a 50/50 mix of almond flour and tapioca when I'm going all-out.

Oat flour is awesome to bake with for a multitude of reasons. It's high in nutrients and is extremely affordable. If you can't find it in the store, you can make your own by grinding raw oats in your coffee grinder.

Oat flour adds structure and texture to many different types of baked goods and stores well. Because it's heavy, don't substitute more than 30% oat flour for total flour. Also, be sure to buy oats or oat flour that is certified GF because oats are often processed in wheat facilities.

Chestnut flour has a nice texture and lends itself well to rich breads and pastries such as those common in French or Italian cuisine.

Montina flour was used by Native Americans. It's nutritious and has a wheaty taste. Since it's high in protein, it lends elasticity to your baked goods but it's also heavy. Montina pairs especially well with Teff. 5

Use Montina for up to 30% of your blend to get a whole-wheat texture and flavor.

Montina is great for hearty, dark products such as breads, cakes and gingerbread but if you're shooting for a mild flavor or light color, use something else.

Buckwheat flour is also a great option. Though it says wheat in the name, it's actually a relative of rhubarb and not a wheat at all. Buckwheat is extremely heavy and has a bitter flavor so you'll want to use it in combination with other flours to temper that taste a bit.

I like using buckwheat because of the texture and structure that it gives my breads, cookies and even pancakes. Use some potato and/or tapioca starch to lighten it up some.

Bean flours such as chick pea (aka garbanzo bean) flour, soy flour or pinto flour. Just like with nut flours, they lend protein to your recipes. They make delicious flatbreads, in particular. Many people with gluten intolerance can't use bean flours because the digestive system doesn't do so well with beans.

Fortunately I don't have this problem when I eat them in small amounts but I avoid soy like the plague because of the phytoestrogens in it. If you're fine with them, you can substitute bean flour for up to 25% of total flour. Adding 1/4 cup or so to pie crusts will add elasticity to your dough.

Beware though that many bean flours have a beany flavor. You can counteract this by using the recommended amount and by using it in recipes with strong flavors such as chocolate, coffee, molasses or spices. **Pea flour** or **green pea flour** is a good alternative because it doesn't impart the taste but it will turn your food green. If you don't mind the shade, give it a shot.

Amaranth Flour is another heavy flour that I like to cook with, especially when I'm making crusts, pancakes, or crepes. It has an earthy flavor, adds structure and browns nicely. Amaranth is extremely nutritious compared to many other flours but you can only use it for up to 25% of your total flour content because it's so heavy. It's extremely absorbent and your baked goods won't rise properly or cook well if you use too much. Add in a lighter flour to reduce the density and water absorption.

Millet Flour is great to use to add some crumble to quick breads, pizza crusts or muffins. It absorbs the flavors of the ingredients around it. It does add a nice light brown or light yellow color to your dish and is just a little sweet. Replace up to 25% of your flour with it.

Tip: Millet goes rancid fairly quickly and will become bitter. Store it in the freezer and don't buy any more than you'll use in a couple of weeks.

Corn Flour is finely ground corn. The only difference between corn flour and corn meal is that corn meal isn't ground as much as corn flour is. In other words, if you can't find corn flour, you can make it by grinding corn meal into a fine powder. It comes in white and yellow varieties with the yellow having a cornier flavor. Both are rich in B vitamins.

It blends well with buckwheat, sorghum, rice and amaranth and makes a dense, rich product. You can also use it to make homemade corn tortillas. Great for pancakes, cakes, muffins and even hearty breads.

Used as a breading, it makes delicious fried fish and you can, or course, make hushpuppies and cornbread.

Quinoa flour, pronounced keen-wa, is a seed native to the Andes Mountains. It's popular in seed form in granolas and cereal because it's nutritious and easy to digest. It tends to have a bit of a bitter flavor when ground so you need to mix it with other flours to balance that.

I don't use quinoa flour to replace more than 25% of the flour in any of my recipes. Quinoa flour is good for savory recipes that involve lots of herbs or even cheese.

Coconut flour is its own animal. I left it for last because it's tough to work with if you're a beginner. Though it's a great source of fiber and healthy fats, it's also extremely absorbent and will cause a gloppy mess if you use too much. Used in small amounts though, it adds moisture and nice texture.

Coconut flour works best in recipes that have eggs and should never be used on its own, at least until you're a semi-pro at this. Good to mix with sorghum or nut flours.

Xanthan Gum is used commercially in everything from bread to toothpaste as a binding agent. In extremely small amounts it sort of mimics gluten's binding effects.

Guar Gum is used as a binding agent and is used in extremely small amounts. It doesn't add as much elasticity as xanthan gum and can cause digestive upset in some people. It's actually sold as a laxative, so I prefer to use xanthan gum.

Tip: Gums are necessary in many recipes since there's no gluten to bind the dough and to give it structure and elasticity. Regardless of whether you use guar or xanthan, add 1/2 teaspoon per cup of flour for non-yeast goods and 1 teaspoon per cup of flour for recipes that use yeast.

As you can see, your options for GF flours are plentiful. My personal favorites are nut flours, oat flour, sorghum flour, corn flour and corn meal. As I've already stated, I'm not a fan of rice flour but if you try it and like it, then knock yourself out!

Don't Skip the Pasta

The idea of giving pasta completely up wasn't acceptable to me so the first GF products that I tried were GF pastas. Since then, several producers of wheat pastas have jumped onto the GF bandwagon and are now offering GF varieties but I haven't worked my way through them yet.

I've tried a couple of different corn pastas but the only one that I've found that I really like is Sam Mills Pasta D'Oro. It comes in different shapes such as spaghetti and fettuccini and tastes good.

Tip: When making corn pastas, stir frequently and don't overcook. As soon as it's done, drain it and rinse it or else it will get gummy and slimy.

Rice pastas are OK too. They cook quickly though so be careful not to overcook them or else you'll have a gelatinous glop that no amount of sauce will make edible. Eww.

What you need to realize is that your relationship with wheat is over. Don't think of it as losing something; think of it as an opportunity to try new things. It's going to be tough not to compare baked goods and pastas to their wheat-based counterparts but try not to. Judge them on their own merits and think of them as different foods altogether. You'll have a better experience and won't be constantly disappointed if you do that.

Give whole, natural foods a chance. You're going to be surprised by how many wonderful flavors you're going to discover now that you're not covering them up with the taste of bread and breading!

Now let's get to the good part: the recipes! I'm going to give you some basic recipes that you can easily modify to meet your personal tastes and preferences. Instead of using the same go-to flour recipe, I've mixed it up a bit so that you can get a feel for different flours. However, if you find a blend that you like, feel free to substitute it.

Also, I'm staying away from including dishes that don't traditionally have gluten. In other words, I'm skipping the "Garlic Asparagus"-type stuff because you can find those anywhere. My goal is to give you good GF recipes to replace those flour recipes that you know and love. Now, without further ado, let's cook!

Finally, the Recipe Section!

Without further ado, let's move on to the good part – the cooking! As you get used to cooking GF, you'll find that adapting just about any recipe is fairly simple. Give these a try and use them as a place to start your new cooking adventure!

Here's a good, basic all-purpose flour that I'll refer to in some of the recipes below:

All Purpose Flour

1 cup sorghum flour (or oat flour)

1 cup potato or tapioca starch

1 cup sweet rice flour

1/3 cup nut flour (I like almond flour)

1 1/2 tsp xanthan gum

If you want to get even simpler, try equal parts tapioca flour, white rice flour and sorghum flour.

Play with it and see what works best for you.

Light, Fluffy Pancakes

If you'd rather mix your own pancake mix instead of buying the pre-made, this recipe is amazing. You'll never guess that they're GF! Experiment by throwing in some berries or chocolate chips if you'd like.

Ingredients

2 cups (280g) sorghum flour

1/4 cup (35g) oat flour or almond flour

1/4 cup (35g) buckwheat flour

1/4 cup (35g) tapioca or potato starch

1 1/2 tsp baking powder

1/2 tsp baking soda

1/2 tsp salt

1/2 tsp cinnamon (optional)

1 T sugar

3/4 tsp xanthan gum

2 cups milk (buttermilk really jazzes it up!)

2 eggs

4 T melted butter or oil of choice

1 1/2 tsp vanilla extract

Directions

Bring milk and eggs to room temperature. Combine dry ingredients well. Add wet ingredients and beat with a wooden spoon or mixer until all ingredients are combined and batter is smooth. Allow to sit while your oiled skillet or griddle is heating to med/high. Don't add your batter to the griddle until it's hot or else your pancakes will be flat.

Pour 1/4 cup of batter for each pancake onto your griddle, leaving room between each to spread.

When bubbles form and burst on top of your pancakes, flip them over. Cook on side 2 for a minute or so until the bottom is lightly browned.

Tip: I like to do one test pancake. If it's too thick, add a bit more milk to your batter.

Yields about 12 pancakes

Buckwheat Pancakes

These pancakes have a strong flavor and are a standing tradition in the Appalachians where I was raised. They're not everybody's cup of tea but they're a nice switch from the norm. They pair wonderfully with a full-flavored maple syrup.

If you'd like to mellow the flavor out a bit, substitute half of the buckwheat flour for oat flour or sorghum flour.

Ingredients

2 cups (280g) buckwheat flour

2 T sugar

2 tsp baking soda

2 tsp baking powder

1 tsp cinnamon

1/2 tsp salt

2 1/2 cups milk or buttermilk

2 eggs

2 T melted butter or oil of choice

1 tsp vanilla extract

Directions

Combine all dry ingredients well in a large mixing bowl. Add wet ingredients and beat until combined and batter is smooth. Let it rest until your greased skillet or griddle reaches med/high heat.

Add batter 1/4 cup at a time to griddle. Buckwheat batter forms little air bubbles when it's cooking but not as much as regular pancakes so keep an eye on how much they're browning so that they don't burn. Flip and cook for another minute or so until bottom is done.

Tip: These go great with fruit and will suck maple syrup right up! Enjoy!

Yields about 8 pancakes

Tender Belgian Waffles

The secret to awesome Belgian waffles is in the whipped egg whites. I don't use yeast in mine and they rise wonderfully every time I make them. Your family will love these so much that you may want to make some extra and freeze them.

Ingredients

1 cup (140g) sorghum flour

1/2 cup (70g) tapioca starch

1/2 (70g) cup potato starch

1 T sugar

1 T baking powder

1/2 tsp salt

1 tsp cinnamon (optional)

2 large eggs, separated

1 1/2 cups milk or buttermilk

1/4 cup oil, your choice

2 tsp vanilla

Put the egg whites in a glass bowl and beat them until stiff peaks form. Set aside.

In a large mixing bowl, combine all dry ingredients well. Add wet ingredients, including the egg yellows, and mix until batter is smooth.

Fold egg whites into the batter gently just until combined.

Set aside while waffle iron heats up.

Add about 1/2 cup batter to your iron and shut. Cook until nicely browned and crisp. It will take longer than wheat flour waffles do, just FYI.

Yields about 6 waffles

Tip: Make sure that your egg whites are room temperature or else they'll take forever to whip up.

Taste-of-Home Blueberry Muffins

Feel free to modify these to make them into banana nut muffins, strawberry muffins or whatever else your little heart desires. I just happen to be a fan of blueberries!

Ingredients

2 cups GF all-purpose flour (see recipe above)

1 cup sugar

2 tsp baking powder

1 tsp salt

2 eggs

1/2 stick melted butter

1/4 cup coconut oil

1 cup milk

2 tablespoons sour cream

1 tsp vanilla

2 cups blueberries, gently smashed

Directions

Preheat oven to 400 degrees and grease (or line) your muffin pans.

In a medium bowl, beat eggs until they're light yellow. Add sugar and vanilla and beat until creamy, about 2 minutes. Slowly blend in melted butter, oil, vanilla, milk and sour cream. Finally, add in your dry ingredients. Once combined, stir in your blueberries.

Fill each muffin cup about 3/4 full and sprinkle the tops with sugar. Bake for about 20 minutes or until tops are nicely browned. Remove, cool and enjoy!

Yields 12 muffins

Decadent Brownies

Nobody should have to do without brownies but with this recipe, you may want to hide a few or it will be YOU who misses out! Seriously delicious alone but during the holidays I like to add maraschino cherries to give them that extra cheer.

Ingredients

3/4 cup all-purpose GF flour (see recipe above)

1/2 tsp baking powder

1/4 tsp salt

1 stick melted butter

2 large eggs

1 tsp vanilla extract

1/2 tsp almond extract (optional)

1 cup sugar

1/2 c unsweetened cocoa powder

1/2 cup semi-sweet or milk chocolate chips

1/2 cup chopped walnuts (optional)

Directions

Preheat oven to 350 degrees and grease and 8x8 pan.

In a medium bowl, mix all your dry ingredients except nuts and chocolate chips together well.

Cream sugar, butter and vanilla together in a medium bowl. Add eggs and beat til combined. Add dry ingredients from previous step. Mix until combined well. Gently fold in chocolate chips and nuts.

Pour into baking dish and bake for about 35 minutes or until edges start to get firm and pull away from the sides of the pan.

Easy Bread Pudding

OK, I'm seriously going to cheat here and use a prepared bread, but it works and it's quick. That's the name of the game, right?

Ingredients

Bread Pudding:

2 loaves Udi's French baguettes

1/2 cup butter, melted

2 cups heavy cream

4 eggs

1 tsp vanilla extract

1/2 cup sugar

1/2 cup raisins

1/2 cup chopped pecans, optional

Vanilla Cream Sauce:

1 cup heavy cream

1/4 cup sugar

2 egg yolks

2 teaspoons vanilla extract (substitute 1 teaspoon for almond extract for an exotic flavor)

Pinch of salt

1 tsp arrowroot or 2 tsp cornstarch

1/2 cup GF vanilla bean ice cream

Directions

Preheat oven to 350 degrees.

Cut bread into bite-sized cubes and toast in the oven until light brown and slightly crispy. Place in a loaf pan. Combine all other bread pudding ingredients in a medium bowl and pour over bread. Bake for about 30 minutes or until liquid has turned to firm custard.

For the sauce, bring the cream and sugar to a simmer in a medium saucepan. Remove from heat. In a medium bowl, combine the arrowroot, egg yolks, vanilla and salt. Slowly drizzle some of the hot cream mix into the flour and egg mix, stirring vigorously so that you don't cook the egg. When it's a slurry, pour it into the remaining cream and cook until it's thickened, stirring constantly. Remove from heat and stir the ice cream in. Strain to remove any cooked egg chunks and drizzle over the bread pudding when you serve it.

Yields about 3 cups. Feel free to double the recipe if you'd like more.

Flakey Pie Crust

Again, if you want to cheat and use a good pre-made flour, King Arthur's is good for pie crusts. I'm just not a fan of brown rice flour so I use this recipe. Since many of my pies require bottom and top crusts, this recipe yields two crusts:

Ingredients:

1 cup (25% by weight) oat (or sorghum) flour

1 cup (25% by weight) super fine white rice flour

1 cup (25% by weight) tapioca flour

1 cup (25% by weight) sweet rice flour

1/2 heaping T xanthan gum

2 egg yolks

2 sticks butter, cut into small cubes and chilled

1 1/2 cups icy cold water

2 tsp salt

3 T sugar for sweet pies. Omit for savory pies.

Directions

Add your dry ingredients to your food processor or to a large mixing bowl, reserving about 1/2 cup for rolling the dough in later. Pulse or stir to combine well.

Add butter and pulse to combine. If you're using a bowl, use a hand-held pastry blender to combine the butter.

Add egg yolks and begin adding ice water a couple of tablespoons at a time, pulsing or stirring in between each addition, just until dough will hold itself together when you squish it. It will look like a bunch of big crumbles, not like a bread dough. DO NOT add too much water.

Shape into a ball and divide in half. Place each half in a large baggie and press down on the ball until it's a fat disc. Place in refrigerator to rest for at least 30 minutes. You can also freeze the dough just like this for up to 2 months.

Remove from refrigerator and let it rest on the counter for 5-10 minutes. Roll it out on a surface lightly dusted with the flour mix that you reserved. I prefer to roll it out on wax paper so that it's easy to transfer. Roll it out to desired thickness. If it tears, just pinch it back together. Roll it up on your pin and place it in your pie plate.

Tips: There are three secrets to a flakey pie crust: All of your ingredients need to be ice cold, you can't add too much water and you can't overwork it. Remember that chunks of butter are fine. Also, don't skip the rest period after you have the crust mixed; it's a crucial part of the process because it allows the liquid to distribute evenly throughout the crust!

Buttermilk Biscuits

As a southern girl, biscuits were a staple of my diet growing up. It was nice to finally come across a recipe that brought them back into my life! Light and flakey, these are great with gravy or with just butter and jelly.

Ingredients

2 cups GF all-purpose flour blend (see recipe above)

2 1/2 tsp baking powder

1/2 tsp baking soda

1/2 tsp salt

1 stick butter, chilled and cut into cubes

3/4 cup buttermilk

1 egg

Directions

Preheat oven to 425 degrees and grease an 8x8 pan.

In a large bowl, combine all dry ingredients. Cut in butter using a hand-held pastry blender until pea-sized chunks or smaller.

Whip egg into the buttermilk then stir into flour/butter mixture. Stir only until combined; one of the secrets of fluffy biscuits is to not over-mix them. If you'd like to roll the dough out and cut them into pretty biscuits, feel free to. I usually just drop the dough by rounded scoops into the pan and pat them flat.

Bake for about 15 minutes or until they're golden brown.

Yields about 10 biscuits

Tips: If you'd like to make these savory or cheesy, just add herbs or cheese right to the dough as you're mixing it. These are extremely versatile.

Hot Yeast Rolls

Light and fluffy, these hot rolls are fit for your holiday table but so delicious that you'll want to make them once or twice a month!

Ingredients

3 cups GF all-purpose flour blend (recipe above)

1 ½ tsp salt

1 T sugar

2 tsp instant yeast

1 cup very warm (not hot) water

2 T olive oil

1 tsp apple cider vinegar

1 egg

Directions

Put dry ingredients in a large bowl and whisk together to combine. Add remaining ingredients and mix on high for 3 minutes. Your dough is going to be extremely wet – this is normal for GF dough. Don't add more flour!

Grease and flour a 9-inch round pan. Using a spoon or an ice cream scoop, add nine scoops of dough around the pan, placing one in the middle and then spacing the other 8 around the outside.

Wet your fingers or the back of a spoon with water or dip in flour and smooth the tops of the rolls.

Cover rolls with a damp towel and place in a warm place to rise until rolls are double in size – about an hour depending on room temp.

Preheat oven to 400 degrees then bake the rolls for 20-25 minutes or until tops are brown. Remove from oven and brush with butter.

Sandwich Bread

For this recipe, I like to use cake yeast because it gives off that delicious bakery smell and seems to rise better too. However, it's often seasonal so I'm writing this recipe with instant yeast. If you get the chance, give cake yeast a chance – you'll never look back!

Ingredients

3 cups GF all-purpose flour blend (see recipe above)

1 tablespoon baking powder

1 1/4 tsp salt

3 tsp instant dry yeast

2 eggs

1/4 cup olive oil or coconut oil

2 tsp apple cider vinegar

2 tablespoons honey

1 1/2 cups warm water

Directions

In a large mixing bowl, combine all dry ingredients. In a separate large bowl, (the one for your stand mixer if you're using one), combine all of the wet ingredients. Slowly mix the dry ingredients into the wet. Continue to beat for 3 minutes. Your dough will be wet and sticky but that's normal. Don't add more flour!

Oil and flour your loaf pan and put the dough in. Smooth the top of the loaf. Allow it to proof on top of the stove for 20-30 minutes or until it's about double in size.

Bake at 400 degrees for 30-45 minutes or until top is nicely browned and the internal temp is 200 degrees. You may need to cover it with foil if it's browning too quickly.

Remove from oven and allow to cool for 5 minutes. Remove from pan and place on rack to completely cool before slicing.

Yields 1 loaf

Pizza Dough

This was one of the hardest foods for me to give up, but most GF pizzas suck. They're either grainy or taste like cardboard. This recipe takes care of that. I like to brush the crust with a little olive oil and season the edges with a little Italian seasoning and garlic when I bake it but that's entirely up to you! This recipe yields two 12-inch thick-crust pies. If you want 1 thin crust, half the recipe or make the extra and freeze for later.

Ingredients

4 cups AP flour blend (recipe above)

2 tsp xanthan gum

1 T baking powder

1 tsp sea salt

1 pack rapid rise yeast

2 T sugar

1 1/2 cups warm (not hot!) water

2 egg whites, beaten

3 T extra virgin olive oil

1/4 tsp white vinegar

Directions

Grease two 12-inch pizza stones or baking sheets and lightly flour.

In a large bowl, mix together your flour and other dry ingredients, including the yeast.

Make a well in your flour and add 1 cup of the water along with the egg whites, oil and vinegar. Mix until the dough is smooth and creamy. Add the extra water if needed; the dough should be almost like an extremely thick batter rather than a traditional pizza dough.

Set aside for 5 minutes to allow the flour to absorb the liquid.

Divide the dough in half with a spatula and place each half on your pizza stone or baking sheet. Using your spatula or greased fingers, press the dough out like you would a regular dough, making the edges a bit thicker so that you have an outer crust.

Set aside and allow to rise for 15 minutes or so.

Preheat oven to 400 degrees.

Bake crusts for about 10 minutes until it starts to brown. Remove and brush with olive oil and sprinkle on herbs of your choice. Add toppings. Bake for another 10-15 minutes; just long enough to get your toppings hot and melt your cheese.

Remove from oven and enjoy!

Chewy Chocolate Chip Cookies

These cookies are moist, chewy and just a bit crunchy around the edges, just like I used to make them before I had to give up flour. Warning: your family will scarf these down just like they do "regular" chocolate chip cookies!

Ingredients

2 1/2 cups GF all-purpose flour mix (see recipe or use Bob's Red Mill)

1 tsp baking powder

1 tsp baking soda

1 tsp salt

1 cup firmly packed brown sugar

1/2 cup white sugar

3/4 cup butter, softened (if you like them chewier, use butter-flavored Crisco)

1 tsp vanilla extract

2 eggs

12oz bag chocolate chips (I like to use milk chocolate, but pick your favorite)

1/2 cup chopped nuts, optional

Directions

Preheat oven to 350 degrees and grease your cookie sheet.

In a medium bowl, combine both sugars, butter and vanilla. Beat until it starts to cream and add the eggs, one at a time, to incorporate.

In a separate bowl, sift flour, baking soda, baking powder and salt together.

Mix flour mixture into the butter/sugar mix a bit at a time until it's incorporated will.

Stir in the chocolate chips and nuts.

Drop by rounded tablespoons onto your cookie sheet, leaving at least 2 inches between cookies.

Bake for 6-8 minutes or until the cookies begin to brown around the edges.

Cool on the sheet for a couple of minutes before transferring to a wire rack.

Yields about 2 1/2 dozen cookies

No-Flour Chocolate Cake (aka, a torte)

I considered this torte (the correct word for a flourless cake) the bomb before I went GF, but now it's a go-to dessert for when I have guests or am going to a covered-dish. Everybody loves it, it's crazy easy to make, and you get to eat dessert, too!

Ingredients

1 1/4 cups semisweet chocolate chips

1/2 cup butter (I use salted, but go with your heart)

3/4 cups sugar

3 medium to large eggs

1/2 cup cocoa powder

1/2 tsp almond extract

1/4 tsp salt

Topping:

Dusting of powdered sugar

1 can Comstock cherry pie filling

Directions

Preheat oven to 350 degrees.

Grease a 9-inch springform pan.

Combine chocolate chips, sugar, salt and butter in a double broiler (or in a saucepan on low) and melt together. Remove from heat and allow to cool for a couple of minutes so that you don't cook the eggs.

Sift cocoa powder into the chocolate and add almond extract. Whisk in the eggs one at a time. Whip until glossy. Beat the chocolate mixture into the sugar mixture until it's creamy and glossy. Pour into your pan.

Bake for 22-27 minutes or until the center is just firm to the touch. Be careful not to overcook it or else it will be dry and hard. Remove from oven and allow to cool. Remove sides of pan.

Dust with powdered sugar and top with cherries before you serve it.

Cream of Mushroom Soup

Many of my favorite dishes contain cream of mushroom soup but, alas, commercial brands have gluten. Here is an easy recipe that will allow you to have green bean casserole (sans fried onions), tuna casserole, and all of the other goodies that require this old-school ingredient.

Ingredients

2 cups fresh sliced mushrooms or three 4oz cans mushrooms

1 tsp minced garlic

1/4 cup diced onion

2 cup chicken broth

2 cup whole milk (or half-n-half)

5 T butter

1/2 cup sweet rice flour (has to be sweet rice – regular rice flour will be gritty)

1 tsp salt

1/2 tsp black pepper

Directions

Melt butter in a sauté pan over medium heat. Add onions, garlic and mushrooms. Saute until onions begin to get translucent, being careful not to burn the garlic. Sprinkle the sweet rice flour over the mixture, making a roux.

Begin adding in the chicken broth a bit at a time, stirring well and scraping the pan to keep it from sticking.

Once you've added all the chicken broth, stir in the cream and add half the salt and pepper. Simmer lightly until it thickens. When it's done, taste it and add more salt and pepper if you'd like.

Note: You can adjust the garlic and onions in this recipe to suit yourself once you've made it the first time. Depending on what I'm using it for, sometimes I like a little more garlic. Play with it!

Yields about 3-4 cups

Gluten-Free Tortillas

One of the hardest things for me to give up was wraps, and now I don't have to. There are gluten-free tortillas out there, but they're hit and miss as far as texture and flavor goes. You can, of course, always go with corn tortillas but I'm not a fan. I'm going to give you two different recipes; the first is a bit more of a batter and the second is a dough. I like the second one better, but experiment.

Ingredients

7 egg whites

½ cup water

⅓ cup coconut flour

¼ tsp baking powder

½ tsp salt

½ tsp pepper

½ tsp onion powder

½ tsp garlic powder

½ tsp paprika

coconut oil

Directions

Whisk all ingredients in a bowl and let sit for 5 minutes.

Preheat 8-10 inch skillet on medium and lightly grease with coconut or olive oil. Don't get the skillet too hot or else the oil will burn and the tortillas will taste nasty.

Scoop about 1/3 cup batter into skillet.

Cook for 1-2 minutes on each side or until brown.

Yields 4-6 tortillas

Flour Tortillas 2

Here's an alternative that I also like. The dough is a bit easier to work with:

Ingredients

2 c. gluten-free all-purpose flour (or white rice or coconut flour)

1 tsp gluten-free baking powder

2 tsp xanthan gum

1 tsp sugar

1 tsp salt

1 c. warm water

Directions

Mix all ingredients together until moisture is evenly distributed and a dough forms. Separate out into balls and roll each ball out into a tortilla, if you're going to cook immediately. If not, cover in plastic. Heat 1 t coconut or olive oil in an 8-inch skillet and fry each tortilla for 1-2 minutes on each side or until desired color is obtained. Enjoy!

Yields about 8 tortillas

The Gluten-Free Guide to Dining Out

Just because you can't have gluten doesn't mean that you're destined to eat salads every timen you go out to eat. Most restaurants offer gluten-free menus and even those that don't are generally willing to work with you if you explain your needs. Here are a few tips to help you make the adjustment to gluten-free restaurant dining:

- Tell the server that you can't have gluten and ask her to let the chef know so that no cross-contamination occurs.
- Ask for a gluten-free menu
- Avoid the common errors such as forgetting about croutons or that there is flour in gravy. Look closely at each component of the dish.
- If you aren't sure about a product (i.e. chips and dip) ask to see the label.
- Ask about the ingredients in a marinade or just order your meat grilled, broiled, baked or roasted with salt, pepper, and herbs
- Remember that most places fry their fries and chips in the same oil that they fry their breaded items in and your food can become cross-contaminated that way. Opt for a baked potato, roasted potatoes or rice instead of fries.
- If a dish seems suspicious when it arrives, don't be squeamish about mentioning it. Just politely ask your server to double-check. If you're not satisfied with the answer, don't eat it.
- Ask if a meats or veggies are dusted with flour prior to cooking.
- Fresh mashed potatoes are typically gluten-free but many flavored instant potatoes aren't. Ask.

A Few Words of Warning

Just because you don't see wheat or gluten on a label doesn't necessarily mean that the product is gluten-free. Cross-contamination can still happen at the factory so if you notice that you become symptomatic from a product that appears to be gluten-free, take note and if it happens more than once, it may be a good idea to avoid that product.

The FDA guidelines for labeling a product as gluten-free aren't extremely strict, though they are getting better. Historically, gluten has been categorized as GRAS (generally recognized as safe) and companies aren't required to list it specifically on food labels. In order to be labeled "gluten-free" a product can't contain more than 20 ppm gluten. As you can see, that isn't the same as gluten-free so just know your body and if you become symptomatic, avoid that product.

Don't be afraid to ask questions; be polite and patient, but don't just assume that something is gluten-free. There's no reason why you can't enjoy eating out just as much as everybody else does – it's just going to take a bit more effort until you get the hang of it!

Eating gluten-free can be tricky but the payoff is huge. Regardless of whether you have celiac disease, gluten intolerance, or are going gluten-free for other health reasons, I hope that this guide has helped!

Printed in Great Britain
by Amazon